In Memory of an Angel

In Memory of an Angel

David Shapiro

CITY LIGHTS BOOKS | SAN FRANCISCO

Some of the poems in this book originally appeared in *Poetry Magazine*.

Cover credit:
Drawing from the Lake Baikal / Vladivostok sketchbook by John Hejduk
With permission from the Estate of John Hejduk

Library of Congress Cataloging-in-Publication Data

Names: Shapiro, David, 1947- author.
Title: In memory of an angel / David Shapiro.
Description: San Francisco : City Lights Books, [2017]
Identifiers: LCCN 2016056580 (print) I LCCN 2017003121 (ebook) I ISBN
    9780872867130 (paperback) I ISBN 9780872867444 I ISBN 9780872867376
Subjects: I BISAC: POETRY / American / General.
Classification: LCC PS3569.H34 A6 2017 (print) I LCC PS3569.H34 (ebook) I
DDC
    811/.54—dc23
LC record available at https://lccn.loc.gov/2016056580

City Lights Books are published at the City Lights Bookstore
261 Columbus Avenue, San Francisco, CA 94133
www.citylights.com

For Don Share and Garrett Caples

Contents

1963

Outside the window you could see
Others looking through the window at me.
Ashes were flying out of the furnace,
Stirred up by the great wind, but no one seemed to care.

It is you, it is you
I keep following, through stations and forests,
And eventually to the sea. How can you look
So helpless and friendly?

For Sleepers

I dreamt I wrote a little poem
Two lovers and of what are they dreaming
Of last night
May you be bright and beautiful
As you are bright and beautiful today
You virgin always living beautiful today
It wasn't I who wrote it
Or made the perfling
Black perfling
Green violin
Disemboweled day
Naked river

IN

Quiero hacer contigo lo que la primavera hace con los cerezos
I want to do to you what the spring does to the cherry trees

— Neruda

I want to do to you
what the summer does
to your wardrobe

I want to do to you
what the e does
to Georges Perec

I want to do to you
what the doorman
does to the door

I want to do to you
what the question mark
does upside down

I want to do to you
and with you what the song
does with the breast

I want to do to you
what the singular
does to the plural

I want to do with you
what the fire escape
does for fire

I want to do to you
what the air
does to the dictionary

I want to do to you
what the prose poem
did for the poem

I want to do for you
what May
does for March

I want to do to you
what the chamber
does to the magma

I want to do to you
reclining what the sign
does to the anticline

I want to do for you
what the wheelbarrow
did for the good doctor

I want to do for you
what the lipstick
does to the lips

I want to do to you
what a naked foot
does to clothed grass

I want you to do to me
what the moss
does to the moss garden

I want you to do with me
what a stone garden
does to Eternity

I want you to do to me
what the curve
did to a diagonal

I want you to do with me
what the wound
did for Thomas

I want you to do for me
what the moan
does for the morning and the dove

I want you to do with me
what the airplane
did to the cloud

I want you to do with me
what the tunnel
did to the tennis ball

I want you to do with me
what the words
did to the song and what the song did back

I want you to do with me
what the ion
did for the dandelion

I want you to do with me
what the tiger
did to the lamb sticker

I want you to do for me
what innocence
did for experience

I want you to do with me
what the wine
did for the kid's kiss

I want you to do for me with me
what the stiletto
did to the eyelids

I want you to do to me
what the violin
did to the tambourine

I want you to do with me
what truth
did to sex

I want you to do with me
what the skin
did to the tattoo

I want you to do with me to me and for me
what the vision
did for the visionary

I want you to do with me
what the bottom and top
did for the top and the bottom

I want you to do with me
what the cure
did for the curator

I want to do with you
what the candle
did to the candle in the night spring bed

A Man Without a Book

1. Poem in a Dream

I would like to comb
the haiku from your hair
vertical braid of language necklace of
words pinprick of a single sound

I work in black and white
much more than you thought.
As I work blindly.
Today is today
these geese.

I am a poet only a poet
and I am no better than any other poet
and no poet is better than me.

Remember architecture!
No client, no commission, "no site" "Oh, it's just an idea."
Night enters the spiral.

2. Death of the Poem

Memory is full
Futility's caravel
She gave me
Love without frills

Full memory
Persian mouse
Crippled asymmetry
"These are all old things"
No, they are not all old at all
        When there was a long king
For every lavender thing
And each did
What she wanted
A post-Parkinsonian poem
A plainly yellowing thing
They seemed too old
And they are not older
They are younger than you
In the lacquered world
The tuning fork above the temple

3. Poem

The trees have sex,
Teach,
Focus.
Tohu Bohu
Chaos in a green light.
Alone again.
How alone I twist
at the end of thought
When illness is forgot
And the speaker

is punched on the bark
on the soft models.
The old abbott looked at us and laughed
He loved electronic gadgets for his tomb.
You were as beautiful

as six almonds
as beautiful as
the naked foot
of the messenger of peace

You sat in a corner of the page.

4. A Poem, Almost

My painter,

my dead painter
ravel, cleave, passion
grief like mine
at home, homeless
dead painter
paint for you,
terrific, bad, white,
dead painter
paint for me
a poem almost
a catenary poem,
colored poem,
primary hands
secondary hands,
pretty, almost too

yellow, green

iridescent gray
Dead painter,
paint her, for me.

Two Ways

There are two ways of writing on the earth:
With an ending or without an end.
If with an end try not to end with oceans.
Without an ending is a poet's delight.

You don't carry a sink while walking in the street, do you?
Fly past me on a lane that doesn't exist!
I saw John Dewey waffling through the night.
He said that poetry was not "about."

It was a starless night—no, there was a star.
Some say it's mold, carve, assemble, or sign.
No volcano is inactive completely, friends say.
And there's the critic with a handle for a pot.

And the young title rising to the roof.
What made you think . . . that love was all "about."
And worse: it doesn't mean about "about."
There are two ways of loving on the earth:

I failed to look far out or deeply in.
You are either one who has lost everything
Or who is going to lose everything.
I saw books roiling in the night like laundry.

It was a new library without a book.
Splitters or lumpers: Now you know what I am.

A Visit

It was a small family party
Aunt Olive who tried to save Dallas
pleased after death to have a park
named after her after death
Terrified I got up off my usual position
and didn't know whether to look or think
Afraid of an encapsulated psychosis
They were quiet: Elaine and Bill de Kooning took a look
and Kenneth so happy, surprised to have a Heaven after all
I decided to accept 10,000 years of imprisonment
if that would lighten my father's obvious punishment itself
lightened by his good works for workers

Meyer Schapiro looked on steadily
as if he were watching "Kings of the Road"
in the scene of excretion
Nothing human or divine was strange, to him
And I had been crying when the 33 recording
of my grandfather's voice played El Mole Rachamim
And I couldn't translate
whom he was calling supplicant
I asked for something faster or fall
Then John Hejduk arrived looking for his wife son and daughter
happy as if he were building worlds again
And Fairfield in painting gear
who had predicted this before
that despite particulars something was the same

and my Uncle Bill born with an open heart
The dead were visiting
in the corridor
I was like a charlatan on TV
finding a smile (long) on the door
or like the philosopher who will always
wake and travel for a table risen
The dead were gathering, I saw them all
my calm father and my mother like two candles
And his father Aaron atheist and good chess player
who taught me to castle early and lift my violin
My father's mother whom I hardly met
walked without me with my murdered aunts
in a nest of keys and locks
They weren't singing

As others concluded I let them go — heard and listened to very little
The dead have been buried off the ground
I only saw them smile
the consolation of the need you'll say and where was Paganini,
practicing so loudly in the orchestra of heaven
where was my young dead friend Phyllis and her flute
And where I just had to look more
Before turning away in terror
A family party parting
Amateur chamber music
The delights of the dead

A Silkscreen

I saw Andy Warhol
Walking into our little park
Hudson Park they've been repairing
Henry Hudson on top

Looking like a wrapped stout Balboa

When with all that ice and dying
Because some sailors get too cold
Andy didn't look like anyone else
But he was
Smoking an extremely long and tuneful cigar
I was going to tell him I had
Never seen him with a cigar before
His guts were hanging vividly with scars by Alice Neel
He leaned back and murmured

David that remark about 15 minutes wasn't me

Maybe a little Eve and a little Reed
Nor the plane food was I fond of
Everyone helped out like gilding the studio
To make it seem by me the robot
And never the philosophers they were worse than the poets
How could I help if they didn't know anything
Like a little fever in Greece
Birds pecking at the immensely unreal grapes
They were painted and now you answer the question

What would you come back as? I said an heiress

But you say you don't want to come back oh that's the best!
I'll have to tell that to Ivan

Best not to be born and second best to return quickly

He paused to photograph me

I said all those Polaroids look like an Andy, Andy

He paused to sign the photo I had taken I wouldn't let you

I stopped you and you said, Are you posing?

With that deadly intelligence

Sympathy for Ron Padgett

I have a certain

sympathy for you today,

Ron Padgett,

And I hope it's not too cheap

Though you have heard it said

Everything that lives

Is holy, certain small things

That are not alive

Seem holy too:

Matchsticks, a purple light,

A cartoon character

A drought

Is good

For tennis

A dome

And lights for night

Song for Open Strings

The liquor store is closed, but open your mouth
The shadows of my old-fashioned windows shut by themselves
Are you holding on to a word? Which word?
They closed the liquor store like French corollas
Open up and play open strings like the moon over a tennis court
As you came from the profane land
Of the moss gardens of Riverdale
By the way, as you came
Were all eyes shut in the ocular orb
First the ocular orb, then the details
First bend your head, then keep your promises
Open up, open the court, open
Years with no locks on the door
Your mind, oh youthfully blind
The way to the sun our friend our enemy is through open
    eyes
Open and tell the truth in time
Then be like language opening slowly in a little sunlight
Open your mouth my happiness and I will put a rose of
    music
Between your teeth.

The Similes

Kisses on the breast
like water from a pitcher

— Pasternak

Kisses on the breast
like a gift rising
like a comedian
attacked by the military
like a brain bursting
with wild gifts
like a book of
unusual expressions
like kisses on the back
of your neck
like the end of specious similes
like a test of much theory
like the Book of Windows
like receiving fresh
paint in the mail
like being fresh to herons
like snowflakes on your eyes
like old friends coming
home alive
like outlandish confidence
in a game
like the poem each line
better than the next
like two surprises in each line
endlessness that still
must end

changing your name and
your religion, too
like including everything
and yet being clear at once
Kisses on the breast
like writing in a dream
and waking up in an envelope

Forgetting a Dream   dedication (to come)

Forget the dream
Forget the poetry received in a dream
Forget New York, forget language
Forget you love violent electric storms

Forget the slit open, opened
Forget a closed cloud, bread and lips
Forget David Shapiro
Forget yourself Buy and sell yourself

Forget the great globe itself
Forget the angels in Silesia
Forget provisions for the trip
Forget that face

Forget eight arms for power
Forget peace Forget restless form
Forget whether it was an actor or a butcher
or a traitor at night
Forget whether it was interpretation or
amelioration

Forget, forget!

What's Wrong with Him

Between pugnacity and song, I choose song.
Between Darwin and the Bible, I choose uh both.
Between plumage and song, I choose music.
Between pugnacity and feathers, I choose feathers
slightly dusting the prayer book
or is it another book an angel reads? about herself?
Between song, pugnacity, feathers and eggs,
I choose the fruit of your womb.
Between Noah drunk or Noah naked,
I choose my grandfather's grapes frozen in sugar water
Between the secret Name and the explicit *puer*,
I choose the mortal secret boy.
Between the tropical bird and the lack of a larynx,
I am lured by the silence of these finite green spaces.
Between ants thinking and sociobiologists,
I choose despair. One whose song was writ in sweat.
Between Varese's tousled and my disheveled,
I choose the wind disheveled in the pine trees.
On the silver summit, I recognized synaesthesia
and so many infusions of blood for my father.
And so many infusions of blood for my father.
Between the suicide and the accident,
I negate accident and am intimate and mural.
Between the peacock and the lack of flight,
I choose flight and always keep my Brecht passport
in my pocket, a vulnerable place to keep your heart.
Between the peacock, the pugnacity, and the song of feathers
I choose the blue eggs scattered in her womb.

Cardboard and Gold

My son said Daddy are there words for everything? I said
You mean the space between
The clouds?
"Yes!" "No!"

Like those who love to think one word will take care of
Maupassant's tree and his landlady.
But it turns out you will get no further than the words that
reach and do not touch.

X uses a hard word one per poem like throwing a true
diamond sale or throwing a ruby on a Corten steel table, a
little gold in cardboard. There is a country where they make
their own cardboard. General words the French love, a
thousand eyes but only one
Kaleidoscope.
Even Merleau-Ponty not specific enough (said Meyer) likes
very pretty exit signs
Without numbers.

Paul Valéry said the world was made out of nothing and
sometimes a bit of that
Nothing shines through. No grin, no cat.

But I think: The world was made of gold, and every once in
a while

Some of that gold shines through.

You. They say it doesn't matter that you can't read the
Book of Splendor in Aramaic. "Just leave it in your house."
Amazing debilitating magic at the door!

If there were the right word for everything, each young
    philosopher
Could dream without sleeping. Using the same ruler and
    we'd all
Have the same measures and ladders without rungs, with
    regular risers.

Music without words: it does a good job of caring about
    you,
X-ray of thought the architect wanted. X-ray for the
    lovers —

I always love to climb that ladder without rungs, I collect
    them. I fight over them, I forgive
My antagonist, Even the wild ladder without tongues. Even
    the word literal is a metaphor.
This is not nothing says the boy to the teacher who could
    care less. Multeity. And if I made up a word
Would it survive like a quark of strangeness? Depends on
    which dictionary you're using, I told
The president of that company. And if you made it up, like a
    rare country?

I loved you in the near distance like a word and rare cool
  blood. What was I thinking?
"You actually think?"

Family Ways

My old dead father put it to me
Women of an "intimate" age
Reconciled all separation
He sung it out

Oh family ways, ah family ways
The song contained a pregnant pause pun praise
Patiently he observed, as the rat jumped out
Patient in music, patient in clay

Patient in love and in death, a satisfied ghost

Song for Chaim

If one saves a butterfly, has one saved the world?

Rabbi says: If one saves one butterfly, even with long wings,
one butterfly that has fallen into water, it may be said
"He has saved the whole world."

If one saves a motley moth, is it the same?

Rabbi: It is valid. If one saves a dirty monkey from a flame,
for example, it is as the saying is: He or she has saved the
    whole world.
It is valid for all creatures, and not more so for the creatures
    who know
how to recite the blessings. It is always valid, even on the
    Sabbath.
It is said: The creatures of the sky are owned by no one, like
    the land.

If one saves the Book from being destroyed, is it also saving
    a world?

Rabbi: God forbid, yes, saving the book from the fire,
saving the book or books from the fire, is known to be
    comparable.
He who saves a book and he
writes a holy book, it should be said,
They have saved the whole world like a book.

If one saves a rose, one rose,
from the garden of your dead Teacher,

is it still appropriate to think
She has saved the world.

The Rabbi was silent and seemed troubled. He replied:

If the house of the great teacher is in ruins,
and the garden is a scandal, and one saves
one rose from his garden it is said even
of one rose: it is like saving the world.
It is also said the rose will grow as large as the world.

The New Song

I designed a hat for you
of distant stars and galaxies
with green fronds and inverted braids and birds
repeatedly singing your name into your hair everything
   else stayed black and white

So I designed a necklace of bright hands
in catenary curves across your T shirt study
around your neck I lit up dark words

For summer I built you a bathing suit
or snowflakes to cool you when you
were hot
partly to hide you partly to trace
partly for shamelessness as stickers come unstuck
where men fight over your navel like a holy city
with wild flowers showing through

I also constructed a blouse of new old butterflies
out of William Blake's old new butterflies not bending but
   flying nearby
The laws of temporariness
I drew on your dress

And on your breast a T-shirt study
of TV jewelry a star of David
but melted down in gold to all the other
faiths and crescents
beautiful as the feet of the
angel of little peace
Now run away and pray
In the violent dress of dolphins

An Owl (in Memory of Gil)

Owl small be enough

The child for all his feathers was a cold.

Oh wow the owl.

The poem the vowels

The owl, look its vowels

That branch for you

Owl, are you an armature vector

And a large step for mankind?

Owl astronaut burgeoning owl is a gift

You give to me give to you

Terrible other things happen.

We stay on our branch.

A hundred eyes

Two will do

Lou Louey Lou

300 species of hummingbirds
But only two kinds of poetry
Yours and ours, the language
And the lost, and only a hummingbird
Can go truly backwards
The poets think they are
The only ones going forward
Oh hummingbirds you pluralists of the southwest
O little rockets
Advance and be not like boys
To a wanton lack of gods
Oh permit yes you the broken resemblances
O migrant lover long may you hover
They praise your skin but not your
Temperament your tempo your timbre
They think you are nothing but intensely beautiful
They miss your hundred humble tricks
Like pricks to wanton.

Grace to be born in blood and fly backwards and without moving
Oh graceless poet I forgive you for one word
Endlessly rocked endlessly rocking
A cradle a single boat is a drunken fly
The gods are throats

Afternoon of Life

The reflection of the bird
   is more beautiful than the bird
When the bird became DNA
It stood up on its own blue blue
He straightened out a bird when he shared
His profile to that of a bird
It took more than 2 lives these tears
   to change his profile to a bird
When the water rippled he had already
discovered the God particle
Is the bird more beautiful a minute ago
   Or about a minute ago?
I stuck to her like a bow taking its own
   photograph protecting the horizon

Tattoo for Gina

Some see a dove
And think Pigeon
Other see pigeons
And think Dove

Some know that all pigeons are doves
Some angry as if pigeons were not doves

But the city lover knows
And I try to reconstruct
The tattoo on one of your many branches

The more arms the more power
I think of you, O pale tattoo
All pigeons, all doves
You friendly cliff-dwellers

Questions for You

What was there to do?

And so I—I forget. I what? Stole the blue jay?

I loved you without a future, without an image,
without reference. What do you
represent, what are you a copy of?

Where is the dragon that David dreamt he drove?

But what is closure when we are so open
And what is lack of closure
when we are so close?

Do you think if the Erectheum could not last that this "no"
    will last?

Who was the sleeper?
Who lived in the shoe?

I know that I love the verb not to know. Do you love it?

Dazzled by absence, by your chair, the chair of Salome?

Men call this pleasure
like a place of rapport
But it—is it bliss
to juggle the body
like a house with great pain persuaded to stand

Do you believe in this fabulous affair

Your hair falls like an inventory on your breast
Fine, in what sense fine? Hmmm?

In the house one asks, Whose house is this? Is it mine?

Cricket, cricket,
aren't you afraid
that you're really too loud?

I saw the red bird too
But where's its wing?

When shall we wake to the recession of dreams?

When will my love come and shut my eyes and kiss them as
    though we played
two parts in a comedy?

But how did the spiders
come out of the ditches
and how did the men
come out of the houses
at the end of the winter
into a soft night?

What are they killing
The sick men for?
They are really on fire

How long have I known you, so beautiful
and not told you about it?

It's morning. Dawn has brought the ships out. Dawn keeps breaking our ships.

Can I tie your hair again?

The Firefly Sermon

There are fireflies in the pavement

In the walls and in concert if not comic

There are fireflies in your hair

There are fireflies under the trees

Birds speak but the fireflies are silent

Beautiful as the bottles in sunlight

Birds must die but fireflies are silent joy

Fireflies are going first on and off

Underneath a dead lawn a firefly is living

Is this what is meant by a school

    They fly at tatami shot level — not very high

Filled with fresh pale glimmers

Are they secretly that blueprint, a saying

Fireflies that might seem Orientalist

One rises like smoke

But some are very close by

Like the truth not being far to seek

It's 8:35 in Riverdale State

And though I have three free tickets anywhere

In zone number one the fireflies are performing

I always loved sparklers

Or *daemon* or lighting up or quietly praying

Or prayer without hope

Or singing in a time of hopelessness

Or behaving like morning poets at night

The one you loved the best but not because you made it

The traffic, the rafter so named I sent the grass away

You don't expect much happiness in three blocks

A field of fireflies, a processional for my sick father

It's darker but then night is modest

Given up women but not fireflies

Who are after all asking for nothing and our retinal cavatinas

A rather delicate bust beautiful in the Bronx

And for all that a man's a firefly

I used to own that big book, *Photoluminescent Phenomena*

One is flying through a broken fence

It's a little pocket park filled with cold light

Above dandelions, weeds, the hands on the partner of
    weather without end, children

but hundreds of fireflies

Don't say the fugue isn't a Jewish form

Oh Steinsaltz, you carelessly contrast yourself

Praise him with the slumped remnants and praise him with
    fireflies

Oh spring up summer fireflies from the dust of the
    Schervier and certain lawns

And your servant to which we lend all parts

In the telling of the tale a firefly could hear my prayer.

Let everything that shines praise the Lord.

The Mysterious Barricades

as Milena remembers the stones of Prague

I always loved the mountains in New York

two seconds ago he loved you more than snow about an
hour ago

how does Couperin matter if they are playing on the wrong
instrument

Two seconds ago even the raindrops were snow

I never believed a person who said I used to be a poet then
they tell stories and later they make money

He was boring because no music was "on" two seconds ago
the bumblebee waltz period perpetual

Two seconds ago I was a poet now blank and black on a
mountain in NY

Yeah you have an octet and an octave but do you have
friends on television

he devoted two seconds to each line if a sestet or sextet it
was like New Orleans without beads (or beads in the
trees)

Two seconds ago I forgot the melodramatic ways she
destroyed my life

All the time I should have been asking You are a poet yes
   but are you anything else?

everything always slightly ruined because of the child
   behind the door

he said quite intelligently that he was nothing compared to
   NOT keeping his work except for two seconds goodbye
   You won the prize but two seconds ago
they
took it away
triple negative
split infinity

A Footnote for David

a footnote is a link and a quotation is a photo and a poem
   can be easily deleted evenings
     Tell me, tell me, delete me instantly, isn't a reference a
     reverence, isn't a name a sign,
     isn't an allusion a profile Eat my profile, old song and read
     for information and spam
     for perhaps beautiful misinformation, as hair and water
     rhyme and think and look, tell me! The hardest to paint
     are hair and water So
   paint hair as water, paint water as hair.
   Even in New York with Basho and you I miss New York
   with you and Basho without which no tree ocean

The Heart of Shelley

I saw Shelley heinous heavenward drowned
The fish were eating the light integuments
Of him stuck to the fire
Poetry and prose six times a defendant
On his forehead the mad
black notes of music to lie on
One pearl that was
The ocular orb
But despite the savage little sea-meal
Blue mentor of the dolphins
Slid by as if Adonais
Was scored for the guitar, Jane again
He was straining
To see all this empty inter-phase
Even the rockets were
Geometries a feast of fire
Scarcely men know
How beautiful Shelley was/is
Not yet notes completely drowned
The heart of Shelley enervated as his garden enormous
Scattered all friends   social songs   all boats
                          like the true singers
                                      singing

Why Rimbaud

For DL

Why Rimbaud, ambivalent boy
 Who renounced music
Geology, murder, adulthood,
 throwing a stone at a stranger.
A butterfly lands on his lapel
 like a Jewish star. No more music.

For the Jewish Objectivists

Seeds or snow
Not everyone can tell
There is a blessing for being blessed
And a blessing for catastrophe
But is there a blessing
For a house split open by
Seeds of snow
So that everyone sees through you
As if you were a grey door

Arte Plena: The Next Movement

I wanted to invent poor art

a movement of one person

in a garage like a cellar

mostly a joke in a maze

But instead I'll invent

another Doretta and another dream

full art full words

You would have liked to

make the world pregnant

to split it open like

the famous pomegranate again

The sphinx again

The Model of a model again

Staircase to nothing again

Oh wet gold full words

history a sea conch

and love a white noise

Oh wet gold crazy love

no breaks within a subtle caress

I invented the new movement

without photographs like

the affair of the whole being

As was said ferocious and

intimate and I invent it

to last

Gratuitous Oranges

There are those who feed only on oranges. — Agnon

Nothing rhymes in English with an orange.
It stands alone, with lustre in a far tinge.
It stands alone, and seems to make a star cringe.

On Saturday it's blue like an orange
Or like a surrealist sight-rhyme in a garage.
Nothing rhymes in English with an orange.

But *rime riche* is rich enough for an orange
Still my doorman sings, Put it away in storage!
It stands alone, and seems to make a star cringe.

Orange replies: I'm drunk from my last bar-binge
Half-rhymes like hangovers suddenly impinge.
But nothing rhymes in English with an orange.

While my wife in French eats one in her nude linge
Playwrights Synge and Inge flap forward on a car-hinge.
It stands alone, and seems to make a star cringe.

Pronounce it orange and then expunge.
So ends the story of the very violet orange.
Nothing rhymes in English with an orange.
It stands alone, and seems to make a star cringe.

Jasper Johns: A Solution

Jar, jess, phon.
Juno, jar Jess. Horn pi.
Raj, jess, phon!

Jess, raj, phon —
Join jar, jess, hun pro.
Jar, jess, phon —

Phon, jar, Jess.
Jess injun jar. Oh pro.
Raj, jess, phon!

Junior, jar, jess, phon
Join jar. Jess, horn up.
Jar Jess, phon!

Join jar, jess. Hop! run!
Jess, phon, jar.
Jar jess, phon . . .

Join jar jess. Hop, urn.
Jess (injun) jar. Hop or
Jar jess, phon.
Raj, jess, phon!

Little Villanelle in China

I understand.
Slowly please.
I do not understand.

Goodbye, Goodbye to the nimbus and the numbers
number two rock, goodbye
to the incessant banker and the half garden.

Where however is silk and where is jade—deodorant
syrup and architectural swallows?
Where are the patient, a locksmith detained
A doctor dangerous like living in a hospital.
Slowly please, goodbye.

Underneath us the ice floes and Baffin Island.
But where are green tea and the synagogues of Shanghai,
Green monarchies. You are allergic to pain.
Goodbye, I understand. I do not understand.

Where is the Yangtze and where the police devouring a dream?
Where is the book I could not bring or buy?
Please bring me knives, irises, a certified person.
I understand. Slowly please—goodbye.

Little Mass

for J. H.

When Bach lay in prison
He could see the fugues in flight
Each necessary note
Converged in an immense (lack of) mercy

When Bach lay in death's double bonds
He cried God is insensitive
He is irresponsible!
To the rotten ornament that was the world—

When Bach slept in the hospital
He could not stop seeing the ignoble voices
He could see his children out simplifying
Old Bach remembered his opponent refusing to play at all

When Bach lay imprisoned and improvising in the dark
He remembered each of his enemies and begged God not to
  forgive them

The Last Dream of John Hejduk

David, I had a dream last night I must tell you—a big
dream. Do you want to hear my dream?
In the dream, a man was a rabbi, and his whole house
collapsed. It collapsed around him, almost on top of him.
His synagogue was completely destroyed. So he took a
journey to find materials
But no one would give him anything. . . . Each religious
group rejected him. Nothing!! Nobody! He had to find
the materials to replace his house, and this is what I am
going to do. Finally he found someone who would give him
something simple: a spoon, a fork. He started to rebuild
his house. That is what I am going to do, David. But first I
must study the synagogues of the whole world. Then I will
rebuild his house. Now I know what I am going to do for
the rest of my life. What do you think of my dream, David?
Wasn't it a good dream?

On a Line by FOH

for Maureen OH

"music must die
but poetry is silent joy"

or I thought poetry must die
but music is silent joy

or architecture might die
but silence is joy without doubt

or poetry must not die
but architecture must die,
that temporary shelter!

Or architecture must not die
But poetry is doubtful joy

An Elegy for Joe Ceravolo

Turn him around
In your wind
In your hand
In his dry marvelous sound
O word

In the ground
In, in
In your round song

Oh word your friend
Formless astonishing and alone

The Angel of Silesia

For Leonard Cohen

1.

We used to say

Give us this day

Or It is Thy will

But God is still.

2.

I like a rose: red, white

And full of thorns

Just Like God

Bloody bride.

3.

The hole in my heart

Cries out

To the hole in God

What's an abyss?

Which is which?

4.

God is little

Like milkweed

They are growing God

Like little seeds

—*after Willard Trask, Frederick Franck, etc.*

Cathedral

And oh the difficult languages!
and oh the easy languages!
Then you left.

When you were a boat
and I was a boat
We hid so much and so well we were finally

unable to find ourselves at all
Yes we left the keys
Your fingers were our cathedral

because everything you did was sacred to me—

Truth but Slant

I kiss you
and tell you how classic your face is.
You chop a dagger in my neck.

I tell you, Never
plunge it straight in.
Always do it at an angle.

Three Songs

for Ron Padgett

1. Dark Cars

Dark sun,

Dark stars.

The whole city drives

in its little cars.

2.

The moon is where God eats

White as a plate to God

That's where angels eat the ice cream

And rain does the dishes!

3. Moon of the Love

Night by night

Love by love

Star by star

And moon like love

—with Daniel Shapiro

The Cherry-Blossom Proof

The Milky Way is shrinking,
So the cherry-blossoms are growing
Larger. You send me longish letters.
Therefore, God exists.

The Full Goofy

for Joanna Fuhrman

First Goofy was lost in
   A circle, unsure, a demi-mondaine
   IN A MIDDLE-MUDDLE

Then garlands surrounded him
   Like a horse with no kisses
   And thriving on petals.

When the sticky snakes ganged up on him
   They bit him as though he were a benzene ring
   Dreaming of thinking.

After all, he was paralyzed in the gigantic
   Rotating Multi-clock
   in the nursery where the black holes are born.

Poem for You

I am jealous of the sand

beneath you
around you
what you see

bright things   gagged lady
sparkling and traveling without luggage
liquidity
before X
you are tattooed on my back   music
dies down

I too grew up in
the soft hands
of the gods

and a little donkey will lead them

Tears, tears, and I know
just what they mean
honeysuckles at night

I wrote this poem for you and haven't lost it

Exterior Street

O put a hand on her hand
On Exterior Street
The day was full of day
On Exterior Street
Moths drank tears from sleeping birds
On Exterior Street
You could think and look
On Exterior Street
The balls of the sycamore were swinging
On Exterior Street
Storing the definitions loading the differences
Why did I still want to give it away
Why not wait and write about that beautiful green sweater
I was a virgin and learnt all about cells from Penelope
Even the private road is exterior
As one said all breasts are beautiful
The Flower this flower is falling over
It will never be more exalting
It will always be more exalting
On Exterior Street

Lag Solo

There's a sign in my basement: Private Road.
There's a sign on my garage: Self-Closing Door.
Between the two, we don't exactly live
exactly die.
In our pocket, dust and ashes; in the other
pocket, images.
We wear out.
And on the gifted machine: a dance-mix.
Or the shadow of a dance-mix:
Dance, She Cried.

In the Other Pocket Dust

Sisyphus had a bad back.
Why? Well, I get up in the morning
And my wife wants me to carry
A big blue bag of garbage
To my son now
Sleeping in a studio in NY. Five flights he will not carry.

Oh I say I'm not supposed to carry
More than five pounds of garbage

And she crosses the border with it

There was a dead body like little Pedro rolled down the
Hill by Buñuel and not the long kiss
Of *L'age d'or* but the dog and dog-dream
In *Los Olvidados*. How do you abandon dirt?
The blue bag also rolls down by itself, full of Pedro

Something little Pedro always wanted to do
It's a cold day. Man is garbage.

Sisyphus has a bad back.

Dirty Pond

What is music

We wander through the park until we reach green dirty
ponds

You buy earrings

You lean your hair over our son

and kiss him until he cries

More!

The Party

for Daniel and Pessoa

Poetry could crash any Presidential party
But Poetry will not crash the Presidential party
because poetry is the Presidential party.

Before the party, heads flowed
after the party, even her lap knees and hair were bitter

Criticize the clothes not the rabbi
you have nothing to apologize for
except certain lies.

The rabbi rises to shake the hand of the prostitute
And Walt Whitman
The President rises

Nobody at the party is strange except the President
everyone at the party knows everyone at the party
And there is Liberty, with the famous gun in her hand!

The President rises
To shake the hands of Poetry

Final Final Final Final

for Joseph

I loved you once when love had hardly begun
The rose the lily the pigeon the sun
Now I love only finials and lopsided en
The white one the fine one a small one the only one
Now it is finished your fine small prayer
All of them meet and gather there

Unwanted Poems

Shyly he asked you if he could write you
    poems
Can't remember her reply
I said Nothing is worse than unwanted poems
In the Navy you may be prosecuted for
Unwanted poems or rather sending
Or speaking through unwanted poems
Poor poetry! I always wanted to write
That poem entitled Unwanted Poems
Maybe I've gone and done that as the unwanted poet put it
But look at the snow as gift: hated by commuters
snow is finally loved and compared to poetry
there's an economy to snow-hatred
Finally, snow lightens worlds like (your) teeth
in your smile as you accept my perhaps necessary poems

A Crown for Ron

Nothing in that drawer.
Nothing in that drawer.
Nothing in that drawer.
Nothing in that drawer.
—Ron Padgett

There was something in that drawer.

There was Buster Keaton attacked by the U.S. military in
that drawer.

There was a blind chrysanthemum in that drawer.

There was your body full as a burden basket in that drawer.

There was my sister sleeping through World War II in that
drawer.

There was a quarter-size violin and full-size in ruins in that
drawer.

There was an almost inexhaustible poem inside the poem in
that drawer.

There was broken neon geometry in that drawer.

There was a gangster teaching Borges to speak English in
that drawer.

There was a feathery paradise and cities at your feet in that
    drawer.

There were four Cambodian dancers attacked by blue
    butterflies in that drawer.

There was my life at my fingertips in that drawer.

All of Indochina gathered to be possessed in that drawer.

There was something in that drawer.

For Her

Adam and Eve

And Emily Dickinson

Were afraid

And hid themselves

As in my cartoon

Bible reprinted

For a son

Is every scar the mark of Cain

Biographers stray

Into that privacy

Like eleven bad pens

Near white paper

Ferdinand Pessoa is an airplane now

In my dream he benignly folded his wings

A Poem I Didn't Write or Pessoa's Typewriter

for KJ

Finally I admit it. I wrote nothing.
Dreams gave me some, lucid dreams.
I approached Kent Johnson's house from behind (no
    Freudian snickers)
and took what I could find.
And amazingly he had already
confiscated half of mine,
which were mere notations of a sick brain.

Koch from 1962 on
spent a large part of his career trying to goad me on, to
    write.
He was so embarrassed he wrote *The Duplications* to cheer
    me up.
But he also wrote every paper at my college, Cambridge and
    even my thesis.
It is true again that the limpid phrase
"John Ashbery's poems are unclear. . ." was dictated by
    Kenneth to shock me out of
pretense and hard words. Kenneth didn't care that much
    about spelling,
as John A did—punctuation mattered to Kenneth more.
As for painters, I tried simply to memorize
every word they said. Later I wrote them down. In a
    different order.
One gave me **clear darkness**. One gave me **ordinary flesh.**

A composer named Bernie, a communist schiz
working on The Shapiro Quintet would come in the 60s
    when I was 13 and help me finish flute-violin duos but of
    course
all of my youthful poems. He did indeed sue me when I
    published *January*
and said that every poem had been written by some David
    Joel Shaper,
a major character in his own dream novel. But Holt would
    not give in. Kenneth reported
a dream where he was changing psychoanalysts and Bernie
    was elected to be the new doctor.
But he is mad—cried KK, and woke up with the title: *Poems
    from Deal.*

Who else wrote my poems?
Well, you can imagine.
I take pleasure in Chekhov's ideal: to accept anything, even
    from a peasant if he/she is right.
I don't always take it out of someone's typewriter, ribbons
    having become archaistic. . .
I try to type on Pessoa's Typewriter, of course.

But I'm likely to use any phrase stray phrase of DL (sic)
    that he took from me. It's possible.
I like to take the very tone of humor from Mitch Siskind,
    my ex-roommate. Note
I don't even speak of the poems my son signed at 10.
I forced him to have poems in his dreams.
He called me: **Chief Poem in a Dream.**
Sooner or later, I used his angels up.

But most of all, I remember Joe Brainard telling me to be
    simpler,
more like the prose of Meyer Schapiro, and I followed him
    faithfully
like music and poverty accompanying Satie on his journey
    to get Debussy to collaborate with a gamelan in his arms.

Fairfield it's true wrote a few of my best nature poems, he
    hated the "dreamy style."
Blake just wanted to give me one or two lessons. It helped in
    a fiery sort of way.
I once thought fiery was pronounced feary and had fear in
    it.

I look back at all my purloined work,
the sonnets by Kenneth, the pantoums by JA, or Ravel?
the obscene slurry new poems by Gary and Gardener, by
    Katie and Koch, too, out of time.
You are in pretty good shape, Kenneth, even now that
    you're gone.

So what remains that is mine? So little.
I had thought life itself had undone so little.
Poems, short and infrequent, I did exhale.
And time to time, I slithered down Eliot's street
to where the synagogues keep their nude hours without
    clocks or bells.

Proust strove me, and after him Franz Kafka.
They taught me to be ambitious and steal the most.
Their tones were wiser than anyone short of Molière,
but he was fed up with my incompetence as an actor.

Saint-Beuve loved me not, gave no poems, nor did the
  addict Corso.
But Allen Ginsberg wept when he gave me his dream poem
  about walking with Kissinger.
His best poem never published. Like the novel about his
  mother.
Half of what I tell you is untrue, but another half and even
  three quarters
are all too true. My mother adopted me as she threw out the
  kitty litter.
My father thought poets should be murdered only by an
  excess.
Over and over I was told that we hadn't died like dogs in
  the Shoah. Untrue! What a family, my cousin winced!
But one day I knew again: even my dear Silence was
  plagiarized from a true composer.
My arpeggios were similar to those minims throughout the
  world.
You guessed it, even my tonality, my tone, my tomes, my
  tone was transmitted to me
by and through and for ancient filters that could almost
  filter you.

No, I didn't write my poems, but I heard the mermaids
  singing, and they were singing to me.

DAVID SHAPIRO is a member of the second-generation of New York School poets. A child prodigy on the violin, he is also a literary and art critic and presently teaches art history at William Patterson University and literature at Cooper Union. He published his first poem at age 13 and his first collection, *January* (1965), at age 18. Subsequent volumes include *Poems from Deal* (1969), *A Man Holding an Acoustic Panel* (1971), *The Page-Turner* (1972), *Lateness* (1977), *To an Idea* (1983), *House* (Blown Apart) (1988), *After a Lost Original* (1994), *A Burning Interior* (2002), and *New and Selected Poems* (1965–2006) (2007). He has also edited volumes of selected poems by Frank Lima and Joseph Ceravolo, co-edited *An Anthology of New York Poets* (1970), and written monographs on John Ashbery, Jasper Johns, Jim Dine, and Mondrian. He holds a PhD from Columbia University and has received awards from the Merrill Foundation, the NEA, the NEH, and the Graham Foundation. He lives in Riverdale, the Bronx, NYC.